Horsey Wit

summersdale

HORSEY WIT

Copyright © Summersdale Publishers Ltd, 2009

Text contributed by Jon Stroud
Illustrations by Kath Walker

Summersdale Publishers Ltd
46 West Street
Chichester
West Sussex
PO19 1RP
UK

www.summersdale.com

Printed and bound in the UK by CPI Mackays, Chatham ME5 8TD

ISBN: 978-1-84024-785-5

Disclaimer
Every effort has been made to attribute the quotations in this collection to the correct source. Should there be any omissions or errors in this respect we apologise and shall be pleased to make the appropriate acknowledgements in any future edition.

Substantial discounts on bulk quantities of Summersdale books are available to corporations, professional associations and other organisations. For details telephone Summersdale Publishers on (+44-1243-771107), fax (+44-1243-786300) or email (nicky@summersdale.com).

Horsey Wit

Jane Brook

Contents

Editor's Note

Welcome to the wonderful world of mucking out, electric fencing and that elusive tribe known as 'farriers'. Horses are an obsession and a lifestyle choice for some and, from Arabian thoroughbred to Shetland pony, there are few animals that are more companionable than one's trusty steed. Even Winston Churchill considered that: 'No hour of life is wasted that is spent in the saddle.'

But don't let these majestic creatures make a foal out of you, because beyond their calm, noble exteriors lie hearts of pure mischief, as Benjamin Franklin once sagely observed: 'The horse thinks one thing and he who saddles him another.'

After chasing your nag around the paddock and being thrown at the first fence you'll be chomping at the bit to get your hands on these words of wisdom. So sit back and enjoy these equine quips and quotes, and remember why your lawnmower on four legs is so special.

HEAD UP, HEELS DOWN

A jump jockey has to throw his heart over the fence – and then go over and catch it.

Dick Francis

Jumping is just dressage
with speed bumps.

Anonymous

There is something about jumping
a horse over a fence... Perhaps
it's the risk, the gamble.

William Faulkner

Nothing wrong with this horse's jumping that a bullet couldn't cure!

Tim Stockdale

Tim, this is the bit you're meant to be good at.

A commentator at the Royal Windsor Horse Show after international showjumper Tim Stockdale was almost thrown at a low-brush fence by an inexperienced horse

Someone once said
that for one to fly, one
only needs to take the
reins. In my experience
flight is often incurred
by letting go of them.

Jay Halim

Let the best horse
leap the hedge first.

Thomas Fuller

My new horse was sold to me
as a real gentleman to ride. He
is; when we have to go over a
fence he insists on ladies first.

Anonymous

Horse riding is a perfect comparison
with singing. You must know
where the double fences are.

Luciano Pavarotti

Half the failures of this world
arise from pulling in one's
horse as he is leaping.

Augustus Hare

Horses lend us the wings we lack.

Anonymous

LOVE ME, LOVE
MY HORSE

A horse doesn't
care how much you
know until he knows
how much you care.

Pat Parelli

When your horse
follows you without
being asked, when
he rubs his head on
yours, and when you
look at him and feel
a tingle down your
spine... you know
you are loved.

John Lyons

If he were a person
he would be my
best friend.

Ian Millar on his world champion showjumper Big Ben

Horses are very forgiving of the
people who truly love them.

Gincy Self Bucklin

—◆—

You don't sell family members
and you don't sell your dream.

Kelly Kaminski referring to when she
turned down $150,000 for her champion
barrel racer Rockem Sockem

—◆—

A man that don't love a horse, there
is something the matter with him.

Will Rogers

Horses aren't my whole life,
but they make my life whole.

Lindsay Stewart

A stubborn horse walks behind
you, an impatient horse walks
in front of you, but a noble
companion walks beside you.

Monty Roberts

Whoever said that
money cannot buy
happiness didn't know
where to buy a horse.

Anonymous

GIDDY-UP, HORSEY!

To ride, or not
to ride, that is a
stupid question.

Brandy Michelle

No hour of life is wasted that
is spent in the saddle.

Winston Churchill

❧

Keep one leg on one side, the
other leg on the other side and
your mind in the middle.

Henry Taylor

❧

The first is to mount the horse.
The second is to stay mounted.

Sir John Mortimer on the two important rules of riding

The left side is the right side, and
the right side is the wrong side.

Anonymous

You only need two things to
ride a horse – confidence and
balance. Everything else you
pick up as you go along.

Allan D. Keating

The horse's neck is between
the two reins of the bridle, which
both meet at the rider's hands.

William Cavendish

There are no handles to a
horse, but the 1910 model has
a string to each side of its face
for turning its head when there
is anything you want it to see.

Stephen Butler Leacock

People ask me why I
ride with my bottom in
the air. Well, I've got
to put it somewhere.

Lester Piggott

If a horse becomes
more beautiful in the
course of his work, it is
a sign that the training
principles are correct.

Colonel Podhajsky

I ride horses because it's
the only sport where I can
exercise while sitting down.

Joan Hanson

There are fools, damn fools, and
those who remount in a steeplechase.

Bill Whitbread

31

I can always tell which is the front
end of a horse, but beyond that,
my art is not above the ordinary.

Mark Twain

❧

If God had intended man to walk,
he would have given him four legs.
Instead, he gave him two – one to
put on either side of a horse.

Anonymous

Experienced riders are not prone
to brag. And usually newcomers,
if... boastful, end up modest.

C. J. J. Mullen

The hardest thing to do on
a horse is nothing at all.

Chris McKinnon

I would travel only
by horse, if I had
the choice.

Linda McCartney

THE BEST MEDICINE

A canter is a cure
for every evil.

Benjamin Disraeli

There is nothing like a rattling
ride for curing melancholy!

Pared

◆━━◆◆━━◆

Sex is an anticlimax after that!

Mick Fitzgerald on winning the Grand National

◆━━◆◆━━◆

The riding of young horses
is an excellent nerve tonic.

Geoffrey Brooke

It's just being around
them that I like best.

Teresa Becker on horses

There's nothing like the
first horseback ride to make
a person feel better off.

Herbert Prochnow

I've always been able
to get on a horse and
go for a ride and come
back a better person.

Mel Blount

O, for a horse with wings!

William Shakespeare, *Cymbeline*

A bad ride is much better
than a good walk.

Peter Grace

There is something about the
outside of a horse that is good
for the inside of a man.

Winston Churchill

CANTER YOU GO
ANY FASTER?

He flung himself upon
his horse and rode off
madly in all directions.

Stephen Butler Leacock

Never ride faster than your
guardian angel can fly!

Anonymous

When your horse bolts for ten
minutes flat, you know to get off
and give up. The question is, how?

Annarose Robinson

My horse is very quick. Sometimes he's so quick he leaves me behind.

Will Rogers

Silence takes on a new quality
when the only sound is that of
regular and smooth hoof beats...

Bertrand Leclair

His hooves pound the beat,
your heart sings the song.

Jerry Shulman

Good horses make short miles.

George Eliot

When a man's mind rides faster
than his horse can gallop
they quickly both tire.

John Webster

When my horse is running good,
I don't stop to give him sugar.

William Faulkner

A horse never runs
so fast as when he
has other horses to
catch up and outpace.

Ovid

If anybody expects to calm a horse
down by tiring him out with riding
swiftly and far, his supposition
is the reverse of the truth.

Xenophon

Definition
Gallop: the customary
gait a horse chooses when
returning to the stable.

Anonymous

A STABLE
RELATIONSHIP

Love means attention,
which means looking
after the things we
love. We call this
stable management.

George H. Morris

Good places make good horses.

Anna Sewell, *Black Beauty*

If you act like you've only got
fifteen minutes, it'll take all day.
Act like you've got all day and
it'll take fifteen minutes.

Monty Roberts on grooming a horse

PLEASE don't
feed fingers to
the horses.

Sign at a local riding school

Closeness, friendship, affection...
keeping your own horse
means all of these things.

Bertrand Leclair

The stable wears out a horse
more than the road.

French proverb

Being born in a stable does
not make one a horse.

Arthur Wellesley

The stables are
the real centre of
the household.

George Bernard Shaw

ON THE HOOF

Never buy a saddle
until you have
met the horse.

Mort Zuckerman

No philosophers so thoroughly
comprehend us as dogs and horses.

Herman Melville, *Redburn: His First Voyage*

No philosophers so thoroughly

Unless you're on the lead horse
the view is always the same.

Anonymous

Horses are the greatest
equaliser in the world.

Will Rogers

Courage, wisdom, empathy
and love, all can be bequeathed
by a horse to his rider.

Charles de Kunffy

Born to live and run free
and wild... kind enough to
share his abilities with us.

Sally Swift

... it brings us in contact with
the rare elements of grace,
beauty, spirit and fire.

Sharon Ralls Lemon on riding horses

The horse lends you his
strength, speed and grace.

Lucy Rees

It's remarkable how consistently
people with horses claim to
have learned much about
themselves through them.

Tom McGuane

The world is best viewed
through the ears of a horse.

Anonymous

There is no secret as close as
that between rider and horse.

R. S. Surtees

MY LITTLE PONY

A pony is a childhood
dream; a horse is an
adulthood treasure.

Rebecca Carroll

If you want a kitten, start out
by asking for a horse.

Anonymous

I should like to be a horse.

Queen Elizabeth II when asked as
a child of her ambitions

When I was a young girl, I thought of
becoming a mounted policewoman
because I figured I could ride horses
and be paid for it – what a job!

Olivia Newton-John

Horses and children,
I often think, have a
lot of the good sense
there is in the world.

Josephine Demott Robinson

I don't have a clue about this horse
stuff other than I really want one.

Marlene McRae

❧

Don't give your son money. As far
as you can afford it, give him horses.

Winston Churchill

❧

All horses deserve, at least once in
their lives, to be loved by a little girl.

Anonymous

A DAY AT THE RACES

A racehorse is an
animal that can take
several thousand
people for a ride
at the same time.

Herbert Prochnow

Ascot... the only racecourse
in the world where the
horses own the people.

Art Buchwald

The only decent people I ever saw
at the racecourse were horses.

James Joyce

Money, horse racing and
women, three things the boys
just can't figure out.

Will Rogers

The racecourse is as
level as a billiard ball.

John Francome

———◆———

It was like driving a Ferrari.

Colin Brown on riding Desert Orchid

———◆———

A horse gallops with his lung,
perseveres with his heart, and
wins with his character.

Federico Tesio

A racehorse that consistently
runs just a second faster
than another horse is worth
millions of dollars more.

H. Jackson Brown Jr

What makes you good is if
you can take the second or
third best horse and win.

Vicky Aragon

Horses have a frog in each
hoof – a thoughtful provision
of nature, enabling them to
shine in a hurdle race.

Ambrose Bierce

———◆———

I never kept racehorses.
They kept me.

Horatio Bottomley

———◆———

The great thing about
racehorses is that you don't
need to take them for walks.

Albert Finney

HORSEY LAW

In the Argentinian
city of Rosario,
horses must wear hats
in warm weather.

Until 1976 the law stated that a London taxi driver was required to carry a bail of hay on the roof of their cab to feed their horses.

In Colorado, Utah and Washington DC you can be arrested for fishing on horseback.

It's an offence to open an umbrella in the presence of a horse in New York City.

In Alberta, Canada, when a convict is released from prison he is entitled to a handgun, bullets and a horse on which to ride out of town.

In Denmark, car drivers must
pull over and camouflage their
vehicle if a passing horse pulling
a carriage becomes unsettled.

Californian post-race drug-testing
laws require that every horse
running at the state's Santa Anita
Racetrack must be trained to
urinate at the sound of a whistle.

A law in Britain
dictates that an
Englishman may
not sell a horse to
a Scotsman.

If you're a woman, it's illegal to ride on horseback down a public street in Raton, New Mexico, wearing a kimono.

Expect a visit from the sheriff if your horse eats a fire hydrant in Marshalltown, Iowa.

It's against city law in Cripple Creek, Colorado, to bring your horse above the ground level of any building.

All pubs, hotels and bars in the state of Queensland, Australia, are still required under constitutional law to provide a hitching rail for patrons to tie up their horses.

HORSIN' AROUND

Anyone who is
concerned about
his dignity would be
well advised to keep
away from horses.

Prince Philip, Duke of Edinburgh

There are only two emotions that belong in the saddle; one is a sense of humour and the other is patience.

John Lyons

The horse thinks one thing and he who saddles him another.

Benjamin Franklin

There are two things you should avoid approaching from the rear: restaurants and horses.

Evelyn Waugh

Horses are
uncomfortable in the
middle and dangerous
at both ends.

Ian Fleming

If a horse stands on you it's
because you're in the way.

Anonymous

———◆———

Horses have four bits of luck
nailed to their feet. They should
be the luckiest animals.

Eddie Izzard

———◆———

A horse's bad behaviour will be in
direct proportion to the number
of people who are watching.

Anonymous

HORSEY FOLK

Horses are
human beings!

A. P. McCoy

There are only two classes in good society in England: the equestrian classes and the neurotic classes.

George Bernard Shaw

Farriers are like cats. They don't like to go out in the rain and they don't come when you call them.

Anonymous

We tolerate shapes in human
beings that would horrify us
if we saw them in a horse.

William Ralph Inge

For every set of horseshoes
people use for luck, somewhere out
there there's a barefoot horse.

Allan Sherman

You show me someone that
doesn't like horses and I'll show
you someone who can't ride.

Anonymous

I'm going to live in the country with
my horse and get a nine-to-five.

Stella McCartney after her first fashion
collection was slated by the press

We become so
wrapped up in
horses that we do
not understand why
everyone cannot
understand us.

Paul T. Albert on being a dedicated horseman

A FOAL IN LOVE

Love and marriage
go together like a
horse and carnage.

Bob Monkhouse

Love and marriage may go
together like a horse and carriage,
but a horse and carriage is
usually followed by manure.

Suzanne Tumy

It's nonsense expecting Prince
Charming to come along on his
beautiful white horse – you're better
off keeping the horse instead.

Julie Newmar

Few girls are as
well shaped as a
good horse.

Christopher Morley

A woman needs two animals
– the horse of her dreams and
a jackass to pay for it.

Anonymous

❦

Treat a horse like a woman
and a woman like a horse. And
they'll both win for you.

Elizabeth Arden

❦

I got a horse for my wife. I
thought it was a fair swap.

Bob Monkhouse

If I had you between my legs for two and a half hours you dear sir, you would be equally as hot and sweaty.

Lady Thornicroft when asked why her horse was tired

A horse may not be able to hold you tight, but he doesn't wander off from the stable at night.

Betty Grable on why you're better off betting on a horse than a man

Whose laughs are hearty,
tho' his jests are coarse,
And loves you best of all
things – but his horse.

Alexander Pope

If a man treats his wife like a
thoroughbred, she'll never
grow into an old nag.

Anonymous

Women, I never met one yet that
was half as reliable as a horse.

John Wayne

Some of my best leading men
have been dogs and horses.

Elizabeth Taylor

A fine horse or a beautiful
woman, I cannot look at them
unmoved, even now when seventy
winters have chilled my blood.

Sir Arthur Conan Doyle

No whisper of
love... could stir me
as hooves of the
horse have stirred!

William Henry Ogilvie

CLASSIFIED ADS

Hack Prospect – Looks nice

Polo Prospect – Short, fast
and can go round corners

Home Bred – Mentally challenged

Nicely Started – Looks good on
a lunge but we'll leave it to you to
see what he's like with a saddle on

Big Boned – Verging on
bovine rather than equine

Elegant – Would break in
two in a strong wind

In Good Condition
– Who ate all the pies?

Good Doer – Until
you want him to do

Bold – Bolts

Forward Going – Bolts

Athletic – Bolts

Needs Experienced Rider
– Needs rider with good insurance

Quiet – Lame in the front

Dead Quiet – Deceased

Good in Traffic/Bombproof
– Lame, blind, deaf and stupid

***

Loves Children – Kicks and bites

***

Well Mannered – Hasn't trodden
on or bitten anyone for a few days

Professionally Trained
– Hasn't trodden on or bitten
anyone for a few weeks

Easy to Catch – Older
than your grandmother

To Good Home Only
– It's quite expensive

To Show Home Only
– It's very expensive

To Loving Home Only – Not
really for sale unless you sign a legal
agreement outlining his rights as a
family pet, write him into your will
and tuck him up in bed every night

Must Sell – Wife has
left home taking kids

All Offers Considered – I
have hospital bills to pay

TALES FROM THE
WEIGHING ROOM

When a jockey retires,
he just becomes
another little man.

Eddie Arcaro

Their bottoms are the wrong shape!

Lester Piggott on female jockeys

———•———

I didn't care about going off
favourite – the horse has
no idea what price he is!

Ruby Walsh

———•———

If a horse has four legs and I'm
riding it, I think I can win.

Charles Caleb Colton

The last horse I backed came in so
late, the jockey was wearing pyjamas.

Joe E. Lewis

The last horse I backed was so
slow, the jockey died of starvation.

Milton Berle

The horse I bet on was so slow,
the jockey kept a diary of the trip.

Henny Youngman

Everyone keeps
asking me: 'Are
you going to win?'
How on earth do
you know if you're
going to win or not?

Lester Piggott

SOUND THE CHARGE!

How do you catch
a loose horse?
Make a noise
like a carrot.

British Cavalry joke

I can make a General in five minutes
but a good horse is hard to replace.

Abraham Lincoln

―•―

It's hard to lead a cavalry charge if
you think you look funny on a horse.

Adlai E. Stevenson

―•―

A young trooper should
have an old horse.

H. G. Bohn

Boot, saddle, to horse, and away!

Robert Browning

Four things greater than all
things are Women and Horses
and Power and War.

Rudyard Kipling, *The Ballad of the King's Jest*

BUGLES AT THE READY

The horse loves
the hound, and
I loves both.

R. S. Surtees

Let the hunting lady remember
that no man ever likes a woman
to know as much about a horse
as he thinks he knows himself.

Anthony Trollope

———◆———

The English country
gentleman galloping after a
fox – the unspeakable in full
pursuit of the uneatable.

Oscar Wilde

I'm weary of the endless
kerfuffle over fox hunting. I'm
told there's a technical term
for my condition: tallyhosis.

P. D. Clarke

The most important gait of
the hunter is the halt.

William P. Wadsworth

Women never looked
so well as when one
comes in wet and
dirty from hunting.

R. S. Surtees

HOME ON THE RANGE

Never approach a bull
from the front, a horse
from the rear or a fool
from any direction.

Cowboy saying

Spending that many hours in the saddle gave a man plenty of time to think. That's why so many cowboys fancied themselves philosophers.

Charles M. Russell

There's something about having a horse between my knees that makes it easier to sort out a problem.

Ronald Reagan

When cowboys are too old to set bad examples, they start handin' out good advice.

Red Steagall

Two things I love most, good horses
and beautiful women, and when I
die I hope they tan this old hide
of mine and make it into a ladies'
riding saddle so I can rest in peace
between the two things I love most.

Epitaph of Russell J. Larsen

All you need for happiness is a good
gun, a good horse and a good wife.

Daniel Boone

There's nothin' in life that's worth
doin', if it can't be done from a horse.

Red Steagall

A cowboy is a man with
guts and a horse.

William James

When I saw the movie, I said, I wish
I had heard the music. I would have
ridden the horse differently.

Eli Wallach

In Westerns you
were permitted to
kiss your horse, but
never your girl.
Gary Cooper

They eat grass, make love, work
when they have to, bear their
young. I am sick with envy of them.

Sherwood Anderson on the simple life of horses

Be prepared to spend several
months of your life in plaster of Paris.

Larry Mahan on learning to be a rodeo rider

Courage is being scared to death
and saddling up anyways.

John Wayne

Never drink
downstream from
your horse!

Cowboy saying

HOLD YOUR HORSES

It's a lot like nuts and bolts – if the rider's nuts, the horse bolts!

Nicholas Evans

We dominate a horse by mind
over matter. We could never
do it by brute strength.

Monica Dickens

There are many types of bits...
but the severity of ALL lies
in the hands holding them.

Monty Roberts

Every time you ride, you're either
teaching or un-teaching your horse.

Gordon Wright

You cannot train a horse with shouts
and expect it to obey a whisper.

Dagobert D. Runes

—◆—

Even the greenest horse has
something to teach the wisest rider.

Anonymous

—◆—

What the colt learns in youth
he continues in old age.

French proverb

You can't control a young horse
unless you can control yourself.

Lincoln Steffens

Most persons do not ride;
they are conveyed.

M. F. McTaggart

Prefer a safe horse to a fast one.

Mark Twain

A horseman should know
neither fear, nor anger.

James Rarey

Ask often, be content of
little, reward always.

Nuno Oliveira

Riding is simply the art
of not falling off.

Maxine Easey

BLESS THIS HOSS

I bless the hoss from hoof to head;
From head to hoof, and tale to mane!
I bless the hoss, as I have said;
From head to hoof, and back again!

James Whitcomb Riley, *The Hoss*

Horses – if God made anything
more beautiful, he kept it for himself.

Anonymous

❦

Heaven is high and earth wide. If
you ride three feet higher above
the ground than other men, you
will know what that means.

Rudolf G. Binding

❦

God forbid that I should go to any
Heaven in which there are no horses.

R. B. Cunninghame Graham

Far, far back in our dark
soul the horse prances.

D. H. Lawrence

A horse is a beautiful animal... it
moves as if it always hears music.

Mark Helprin

When I looked at life from the
saddle, it was as near to heaven
as it was possible to be.

Daisy Greville

One of the
earliest religious
disappointments
of a young girl's
life devolves upon
her unanswered
prayer for a horse.

Phyllis Theroux

In the beginning, God created
heaven, earth and horses. The Lord
should have quit while he was ahead.

Dandi Daley Mackall

I'd sooner have that horse
happy than go to heaven.

Enid Bagnold

When I die I want fine fat-arsed
horses to take me to the cemetery,
not skinny old knackers.

Christine English

There is a touch of
divinity even in brutes,
and a special halo
about a horse, that
should forever exempt
him from indignities.

Herman Melville, *Redburn: His First Voyage*

HORSEPOWER

No matter how much
machinery replaces
the horse, the work...
is still measured
in horsepower.

Marguerite Henry

I prefer a bike to a horse. The brakes are more easily checked.

Lambert Jeffries

❦

People on horses look better than they are. People in cars look worse than they are.

Marya Mannes

❦

They say they can make fuel from horse manure – now, I don't know if your car will be able to get thirty miles to the gallon, but it's sure gonna put a stop to siphoning.

Billie Holiday

Planes, automobiles, trains...
they're great but when it comes
to getting the audience's heart
going, they can't touch a horse.

John Wayne

When will they make a tractor
that can furnish the manure
for farm fields and produce a
baby tractor every spring?

George Rupp

The wagon rests in winter, the sleigh in summer, the horse never.

Yiddish proverb

If horses knew their strength we should not ride anymore.

Mark Twain

There is nothing in which a horse's power is better revealed than in a neat, clean stop.

Michel De Montaigne

TEN LESSONS FROM
YOUR HORSE

Think you're a little tense? I'm the
only one around here who seems
to know that there are dragons in
the woods and that we really should
be heading for home. NOW!!

Think you're short of temper?
How about a chase around
the paddock for an hour or so
before I let you catch me?

———◆———

Think you're short-sighted? There
are plenty of places in those
forty acres that I can hide if you
really want to test your eyes.

———◆———

Think you've got quick reactions?
How about I show you how
quickly a herbivore can kick
compared to an omnivore.

Think you're superior? Just remind me who's mucking out whose stable?

Think you're worried? How
about playing a game? It's
called 'mystery lameness'.

———◆———

Think you're a little self-absorbed?
I've got plenty of ways to make sure
that you're paying full attention.

———◆———

Feeling arrogant? Fancy
a demonstration of what a
1,200-lb yahoo event horse can
do with enough inspiration?

Feeling lonely? Let's get
together for breakfast... and
elevenses, lunch and dinner.

—◆—

Think you're financially secure? Let
me introduce you to my favourite
vet, farrier and equine chiropractor.

WHY THE LONG FACE?

People expect me to
neigh, grind my teeth,
paw the ground and
swish my tail – none
of which is easy.

Princess Anne

Marry me and I'll never
look at another horse.

Groucho Marx

The one thing I do not want
to be called is First Lady. It
sounds like a saddle horse.

Jackie Kennedy

The horse stopped with a
jerk, and the jerk fell off.

Jim Culleton

❦

If an ass goes travelling he will
not come home a horse.

Thomas Fuller

❦

Princess Anne looks like a
horse just shit in her handbag.

Billy Connolly

A camel is a horse designed
by a committee.

Sir Alec Issigonis

I've spent my whole life being told
I have a face like a horse. You are
just what you are, aren't you?

Jeremy Paxman

A horse may be coaxed to drink,
but a pencil must be lead.

Stan Laurel

If the world were a truly rational
place, men would ride side-saddle.

Rita Mae Brown

I'd horsewhip you
if I had a horse.

Groucho Marx

ALL THE PRETTY
HORSES

Ask me to show you
poetry in motion, and I
will show you a horse.

Anonymous

This is really a lovely horse and I speak from personal experience since I once mounted her mother.

Ted Walsh

For my horse is a dream, a dream of the making.

Lindsay Turcotte

A horse is wonderful by definition.

Piers Anthony

———◆———

Breed the best to the best
and hope for the best.

Anonymous

———◆———

If you have seen nothing but the
beauty of their markings and limbs,
their true beauty is hidden from you.

Al-Mutanabbi

I am still under the impression
that there is nothing alive quite so
beautiful as a thoroughbred horse.

John Galsworthy

Men are generally more careful
of the breed of their horses and
dogs than of their children.

William Penn, *Some Fruits of Solitude*

Horses are living
works of art.

Robert M. Miller

The eternal and wonderful sight of
horses at liberty is magical to watch.

Bertrand Leclair

I can look the whole day with
delight upon a handsome picture,
though it be but of a horse.

Sir Thomas Browne

But why discourse upon the
virtues of the horse? They are
too numerous to tell save when
you have a horse to sell!

Josh Billings

HORSEPLAY

Three-day eventing...
gruelling test of
elegance, skill and
endurance that
makes both horse
and rider appreciate
the fourth day!

Anonymous

It's like playing golf from a helicopter.

Jilly Cooper on the game of polo

A polo handicap is a person's
ticket to the world.

Winston Churchill

You are a dear soul who plays polo,
and I am a poor Pole who plays solo.

Ignacy Jan Paderewski in conversation
with a polo player

Dressage? Stressage!

Katerina Cox

Poll flexion, not Pull flexion.

Dr Thomas Ritter

All King Edward's Horses
Canter Many Big Fences

Mnemonic for the A-K-E-H-C-M-B-F
letters around a dressage arena

If you want to end a drought
or dry spell, wear a new jacket
and hat to an outdoor arena.

Anonymous

Had I known about breathing...
how much simpler my competitive
riding life would have been!

Victor Hugo-Vidal

Just because it's called Prix St George doesn't mean that it's a race... nor are there any dragons involved.

Rebecca Beaves

The Olympics are for everyone,
not just someone who happens
to own a dancing horse.

Glenn Wool

I wanted to ride at the
Olympics, not present it!

Clare Balding

IN HORSE I TRUST

It is the difficult
horses that have the
most to give you.

Lendon Gray

It takes a good deal
of physical courage
to ride a horse. This,
however, I have. I
get it at about forty
cents a flask, and
take it as required.

Stephen Butler Leacock

I have a new horse. I get her to come
to me from half a mile away with
just a simple call. That's because
she knows that when she's with me,
she's taken care of. She trusts me.

Russell Crowe

Everything depends on
me and my horse.

Mamie Francis

Although a riding horse often
weighs half a ton it can be led
about by a piece of string.

Marguerite Henry

There are times when you can
trust a horse, times when you can't,
and times when you have to.

Anonymous

If the horse does not enjoy his
work, his rider will have no joy.

Hans-Heinrich Isenbart

EQUINE PHILOSOPHY

To err is human,
to whinny equine.

Cheryl Farner

Ride the horse in the
direction it's going.

Werner Erhard

❦

One must plough with
the horses one has.

German proverb

❦

Qui me amat, amat et equum meam.
Love me, love my horse.

Latin proverb

One can't shoe a
running horse.

Dutch proverb

A dog may be man's best friend,
but the horse wrote history.

Anonymous

A mule is just like a horse,
but even more so.

Pat Parelli

It's what you learn after you
know it all that's important.

Jimmy Williams

You're not working on your horse,
you're working on yourself.

Ray Hunt

The horses of hope gallop, but
the asses of experience go slowly.

Russian proverb

One may lead a horse to water,
twenty cannot make him drink.

Christina Rossetti, *The Goblin Market*

THE HORSE
KNOWS BEST

If your horse doesn't care,
you shouldn't either.

Linsy Lee

❧

Dear to me is my bonnie
white steed; oft has he helped
me at a pinch of need.

Sir Walter Scott

If you don't know where you're
going, the horse will decide for you.

Anonymous

———•———

If your horse says no, you either
asked the wrong question, or
asked the question wrong.

Pat Parelli

———•———

... sensible enough to get rid of
its rider at an early stage and
carry on unencumbered.

Clive James' definition of a loose horse

Whoever said a horse
was dumb, was dumb.

Will Rogers

Horses may be wrong in their truthfulness – they may report a brace of flying dragons overhead.

Helen Husher

When I hear somebody talk about a horse being stupid, I figure it's a sure sign that animal has outfoxed them

Tom Dorrance

Do not underestimate a horse's pride, or he will dent yours.

Anonymous

ODDS AND EVENS

Horse racing is
animated roulette.

Roger Kahn

Horse sense is the thing
a horse has which keeps it
from betting on people.

W. C. Fields

Never bet on a sure thing unless
you can afford to lose.

Anonymous

Nobody has ever bet enough
on a winning horse.

American proverb

I know nothing about racing and any money I put on a horse is a sort of insurance policy to prevent it winning.

Frank Richardson

One way to stop a runaway horse is to bet on him!

Jeffrey Bernard

Horses have never hurt anyone yet, except when they bet on them.

Stuart Cloete

There are three easy
ways of losing money –
racing is the quickest,
women the most
pleasant, and farming
the most certain.

Lord Amherst

MY KINGDOM
FOR A HORSE!

Gipsy gold does not
chink and glitter. It
gleams in the sun and
neighs in the dark.

Claddagh Gypsy saying

A horse is worth
more than riches.

Spanish proverb

A horse, a horse, my
kingdom for a horse!

William Shakespeare, *Richard III*

I used to have money,
now I have horses.

Anonymous

Who buys a horse buys care.

Spanish proverb

My father hated selling horses
– he was always afraid the good
one was going to get away.

Robert Lehman

A NOBLE STEED

A prince is never
surrounded by as
much majesty on his
throne as he is on
a beautiful horse.

William Cavendish

A fine man on a fine horse is the
noblest bodily object in the world.

G. K. Chesterton

Nobility without conceit, friendship
without envy, beauty without vanity.
A willing servant yet never a slave.

Ronald Duncan

My horse, without peer.

Robert Browning

Wherever man has left his footprint
in the long ascent from barbarism
to civilisation we will find the hoof
print of the horse beside it.

John Trotwood Moore

Honour lies in the mane of a horse.

Herman Melville

When you are on a great horse, you have the best seat you will ever have.

Winston Churchill

———

In my opinion, a horse is the animal to have. Eleven-hundred pounds of raw muscle, power, grace and sweat between your legs – it's something you just can't get from a pet hamster.

Anonymous

This most noble beast is the
most beautiful, the swiftest
and of the highest courage
of domesticated animals.

Pedro García Conde

His neigh is like the bidding
of a monarch, and his
countenance enforces homage.
He is indeed a horse...

William Shakespeare, *King Henry V*

The horse is God's
gift to mankind.

Arabian proverb

PARTING SHOTS

Horse falls are just you and the ground – ninety per cent the ground!

Vic Armstrong

Your horse probably won't
go too far without you if there
is some tasty grass around
~ remember to keep some handy
if you anticipate falling off.

Lesley Ward

They say princes learn no art
truly but the art of horsemanship.
The reason is the brave beast
is no flatterer. He will throw a
prince as soon as his groom.

Ben Jonson

How many times you have to fall off
before becoming a great rider? As
surely I am nearly there by now!

Cheryl Keizer

———◆———

There comes a point in every
rider's life when he has to sit
back and wonder, am I nuts?

Kelly Stewart

———◆———

I only owe it to the horse's good
nature that I am not thrown off...

Ludwig Wittgenstein

A horse which stops
dead just before
a jump and thus
propels its rider into a
graceful arc provides
a splendid excuse for
general merriment.

Prince Philip

It is not enough for a man to know
how to ride; he must know how to fall.

Mexican proverb

When I'm approaching a water
jump, with dozens of photographers
waiting for me to fall in, and
hundreds of spectators wondering
what's going to happen next, the
horse is just about the only one
who doesn't know I am Royal!

Princess Anne

Misfortunes arrive on horseback
and depart on foot.

French proverb

I thought that movies were
made by the cowboys and that
they just said, 'Okay, you fall
off the horse this time.'

John Sayles

Our greatest glory is not in never
falling, but in rising every time we fall.

Confucius

When you're young
and you fall off
a horse, you may
break something.
When you're my
age, you splatter.

Roy Rogers

Have you enjoyed this book?
If so, why not write a review
on your favourite website?

Thanks very much for buying
this Summersdale book.

www.summersdale.com